74 WAYS

to

INCREASE

Sales & Profits

by Leaps & Bounds

Kathy Jiamboi

GROWING YOUR PRACTICE

 On behalf of Creativedge Marketing, I would like to thank you for your interest in *74 Ways to Increase Your Sales & Profits by Leaps & Bounds.* I hope by the time you finish reading this book, you will be thanking us for the information it provides.

Growing Businesses is What We Do.
The fundamentals of business success lie in a well thought out marketing system. This book contains a collection of some of the expert marketing "Tips, Trends and Tactics" we deliver to our clients to help grow their businesses.

You will find "The 74 Ways" useful to both those starting out in business and those already in business. This book will either give you new ideas or remind you of those ideas and concepts you may have forgotten.

We wish you much success with your practice!

Kathy Jiamboi
Creativedge Marketing

#1
MARKET DIFFERENTLY

If you go along with your industry standards and market your business the same way your competitors do, you will get the same average results over and over again.

To be more effective with your advertising, don't do what everyone else in your industry is doing. That just dilutes the message. Take time to think of things you can do that may be different or consider something another industry does that has been successful and adapt it to your business.

Different and unconventional marketing will attract attention and new business.

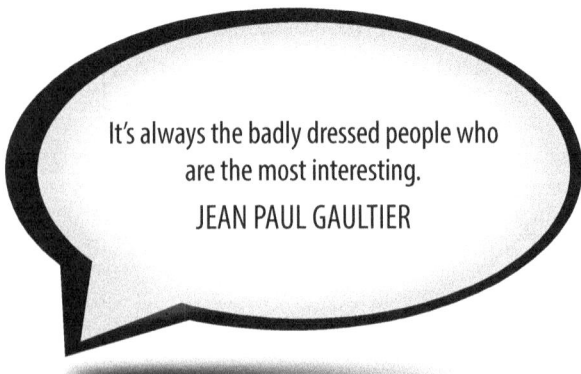

It's always the badly dressed people who are the most interesting.

JEAN PAUL GAULTIER

#2
PREMIUM OPTIONS

Many practices underestimate the price flexibility of their product or service. Without a doubt there is a percentage of your patients who will gladly purchase a premium option of what you sell if you offer it to them.

Here are some examples of premium products people buy frequently without price being a factor - Evian water, Starbucks Mocha Latte, Godiva chocolate, Viking stoves, Sub Zero refrigerators, Williams-Sonoma products. For each one of these products you can easily find less expensive versions.

Work to create premium options in your product or service offerings.

> Customers don't always know what they want. The decline in coffee-drinking was due to the fact that most of the coffee people bought was stale and they weren't enjoying it. Once they tasted ours and experienced what we call "the third place".. a gathering place between home and work where they were treated with respect.. they found we were filling a need they didn't know they had.
>
> HOWARD SCHULTZ

#3
IMPLEMENTING FAST

Speed is a definite factor in the success of a business. Speed gives your business momentum and momentum has a way of giving things a life of their own.

The time it takes you to go from a marketing idea to actual implementation of that idea will have much to do with your bottom line. The longer it takes to implement ideas, the more costly the idea becomes both in terms of not having the idea on the market and the time spent on countless revisions.

When going from idea to implementation, institute tight deadlines and high expectations to create positive pressure to keep you moving toward getting those ideas in place more quickly.

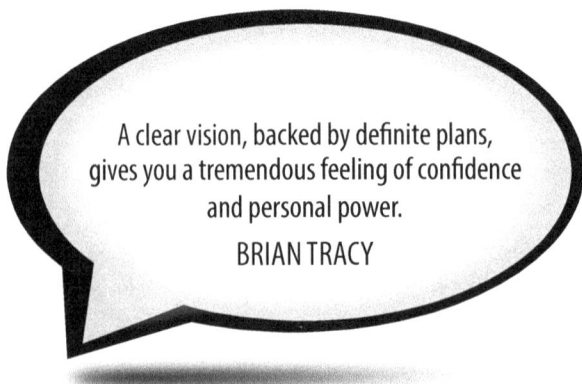

A clear vision, backed by definite plans, gives you a tremendous feeling of confidence and personal power.

BRIAN TRACY

#4
REFERRALS RULE

The easiest customer to sell is a previous customer. The second easiest customer to sell is a referral from a previous customer.

Six good reasons to have a referral program—

1. A referral is basically a pre-sold customer
2. A referral is the easiest and fastest way to increase business
3. A referral costs far less to acquire
4. A referral is less price resistant
5. A referral is more likely to refer since someone referred them
6. A referral is less likely to complain

The reason a customer refers another customer to you is because they believe their friend or business associate will truly benefit from your product or service.

A thank you note or gift is a great way to show appreciation for a referral but it will not be the reason someone refers business to you.

Excellent service is the most influential factor in getting referrals.

A referral program does not necessarily have to have an incentive attached to it to make it work, but it may make it a bit easier to ask for a referral when there is a reward involved.

#5
PURPOSE AND DESIGN OF AN AD

The purpose of an ad should not be to brand your product or service.

Often times you will see ads that do just that. Name of the company large at the top of the ad, a few features about their product or service and contact information at the bottom.

The purpose of your ad should be to generate leads or new prospects. In order to get these prospects to call, you must give them a compelling reason why they need your product or service and that reason must match the needs of the audience receiving the message.

Before creating your ad, know who your audience is, then craft the offer to suit their needs.

How often should you change the look of your ad?

Many people feel their prospects will become bored with their ads and to prevent that from happening, they need to keep changing the appearance of them. Or, they feel they are not being creative if they continue using the same ad over and over.

The time to change your ad is when the ad stops producing the prospects you need.

Since your ad is designed to locate prospects, your message will be brand new to someone who has not responded. It may be old to those who have responded but these are not the people you are trying to attract.

#6
HAVE A MARKETING SYSTEM

McDonald's, Walmart and Disney all share a common trait—systems.

Without systems in place you will spend your time reacting to everything on a constant basis and consume much time and energy.

Of all systems, a marketing system can be the most valuable.

Create a system, for each of these steps to a sale:
- Lead Generation
- Sales Presentation
- Sales Process
- Follow Up

When you have systems it leaves no question as to what to do next and when everyone follows the same system it improves communication, customer satisfaction and customer retention.

Business has only two functions - marketing and innovation.
MILAN KUNDERA

#7
REASONS FOR LACK OF RESPONSE

Because they didn't respond to your offer, doesn't mean they never will. But many think a lack of response means just that.

Consider these reasons why people don't respond immediately—

1. They were out of town.
2. They haven't been able to get to it.
3. They have no trust in your company yet.
4. They need more information.
5. They are not interested right now.
6. Their budget is spent for now.
7. They didn't understand your offer.
8. Your offer was not compelling enough.

The list could go on.

The point is to keep following up with as many offers tweaking your message along the way to give them every opportunity to become your patient.

#8
CRAFTING A GREAT OFFER

1. Make sure your offer is clear and people can understand it. If it is confusing it will affect your response rate.

2. Make sure your offer has value. People want to feel they are getting something worthy.

3. Offer some type of discount or premium/free gift with the purchase.

4. State the reason for the offer such as - introductory rate anniversary sale, limited time available, new to the neighborhood special, etc.

5. Give a reason to take action - expiration date, limited availability.

6. Make sure there is a definite call to action. Call now for an Appointment, Schedule an Appointment at our Website. Whatever you want the prospect to do, tell them.

7. Offer a guarantee. This will remove some of their fear of purchase.

8. Sell benefits not features. Benefits will give your product or service value.

#9
USE CASE STUDIES

Consider developing a brochure or flyer from the patient's viewpoint and let the patient sell your product.

Use case studies to showcase how your product or service benefitted your patients. This is a great way to sell your product and its capabilities.

It not only makes you the expert in your field, but proves your practice to be a problem solver and a practice that cares about helping its patients.

When patients can easily see how the needs of others have been met, they will be more receptive to how you might be able to help them.

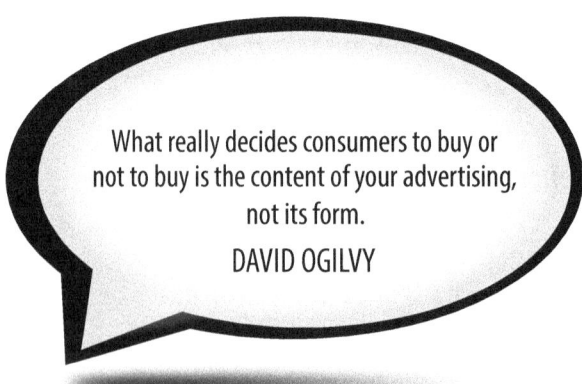

What really decides consumers to buy or not to buy is the content of your advertising, not its form.

DAVID OGILVY

#10
YOUR BUSINESS CARD AS A SELLING TOOL

Business cards are sometimes an under-utilized marketing tool. If you are not using the BACK of your card, you are wasting space.

The space on the back can be used for valuable information such as your Unique Selling Proposition (USP). Other uses could be important dates, emergency phone numbers, a sports schedule, or any other helpful information.

Be sure to have your cards wherever you go-your car, your wallet/purse, at home, etc. You never know when you might need one or where you will find your next patient.

Consider using business cards as a mini brochure to market different products and services. It's a low cost way to provide specific information to a prospect.

Put benefits about the product/service on the front and a coupon or special offer on the back. Don't forget your contact info...

#11
NEWSLETTERS ARE A MUST

A printed monthly newsletter is a must for every practice.

Newsletters:
- Build relationships with your patients
- Entice patients to spend more money
- Create patients loyalty
- Keep your practice at the top of your patient's mind
- Are a way to let patients know what's going on in your practice
- Are a avenue to offer patients specials and discounts
- Differentiate you from your competition
- Are a terrific referral source

Newsletters are an inexpensive way to keep your company in the forefront of your patient's mind.

Here are more very good benefits for sending a monthly newsletter.

They will help you get "tough" patients. While you wouldn't want to send a newsletter to a cold prospect, sending it to those who you are trying to get is a wise decision. It is your chance to communicate your success and your prospects will be able to evaluate you before making a commitment.

People read newsletters. People throw away a lot of other mail. As long as your newsletter is easy to read and offers helpful information, it will get read.

#12
DON'T GIVE UP

How many times do you follow up with a prospective patient before giving up?

Many people quit after one try. They feel if the patient does not buy right then, they are not a serious buyer.

Nothing could be further from the truth and more costly to a practice. As we mentioned in a previous "way" in this book, there are countless reasons why people don't respond right away. The same holds true for buying.

It is said that 80% of all sales occur on the 5th or subsequent sales call after an initial sales presentation. If you stop your follow up after two or three calls, you may be missing out.

Don't give up!

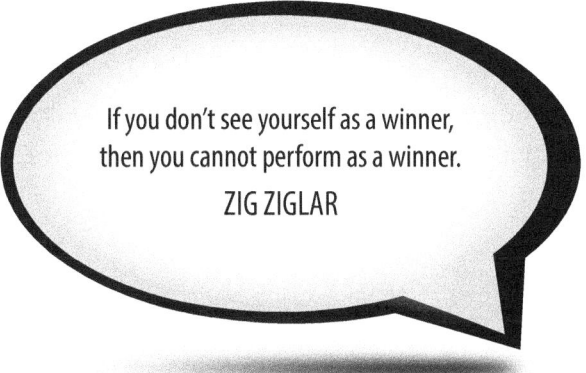

If you don't see yourself as a winner, then you cannot perform as a winner.

ZIG ZIGLAR

#13
GET YOUR MAIL OPENED

Here are the best tips for getting your mail piece opened.

1. Handwrite the name and address.
2. Use a live stamp.
3. Use a different color envelope.
4. Use a different size envelope, such as a greeting card size.
5. Make it dimensional by enclosing a giveaway or putting it in a box or tube.

It may cost more to do these things but the increase in actually getting your piece opened versus your prospect not even seeing it should be enough to encourage you to do so.

Creating dimensional mail pieces is probably the best way to get your prospect to open your mail. Everyone wants to know what's in the box or what's in that lumpy envelope.

It is said that bulky mail will get you double the response rate of that of flat mail.

Even though the postage is more on this type of mail, don't let it dissuade you from giving it a try. Your return should far outweigh the cost if it is executed properly.

#14
COMMUNICATION

Open communication is one of the best ways to keep your new patient from going to your competition.

Consider sending a survey for comments and suggestions following a recent visit to your practice.

Even though you may discover some dissatisfied patients, better you know what they think early on, and take the necessary steps for improvement; rather than never hearing from them again, or worse yet, having them spreading the word about their dissatisfaction to their friends and family.

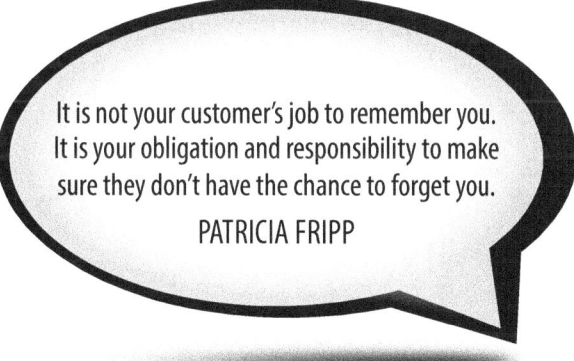

It is not your customer's job to remember you. It is your obligation and responsibility to make sure they don't have the chance to forget you.

PATRICIA FRIPP

#15
BUILD LOYALTY

Keep your new patient loyal by–

- Sending thank you notes
- Sending birthday cards
- Sending holiday cards
- Sending any or all of the above with a coupon or gift certificate to give them the opportunity to purchase from you again.

If the purchase is a larger one, you may want to consider sending a gift along with your thank you note.

Recognizing and appreciating your patients can be a powerful and inexpensive way to market your practice.

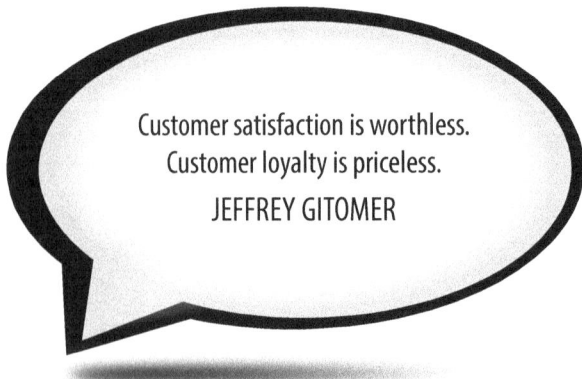

Customer satisfaction is worthless.
Customer loyalty is priceless.
JEFFREY GITOMER

#16
CONSISTENCE IN MARKETING

Continuity in your marketing is vital to on-going sales.

If you are consistent with your message and use various ways to get your message to your prospects, you will be more likely to be remembered when it's time to buy.

Investigate all the ways you can get to your prospect, such as trade shows, direct mail, faxing, emailing, advertising in targeted publications, radio, tv, publishing articles, sending newsletters, in-person visits, blogging, web sites, press releases, etc.

> I avoid clients for whom advertising is only a marginal factor in their marketing mix. They have an awkward tendency to raid their advertising appropriations whenever they need cash for other purposes.
>
> DAVID OGILVY

#17
PRESENTATION TACTIC

Here is a way to present your practice to those prospects who say they are satisfied with their current doctor.

When you present your product or service show it in a way where your product/service will work well WITH their current doctor.

Then, highlight a specific benefit your practice offers that you know their current practice doesn't offer. (This benefit has to be something of value to your prospect.)

This will elevate your product/service without having to say anything negative about your competition, and hopefully move you to a new patient.

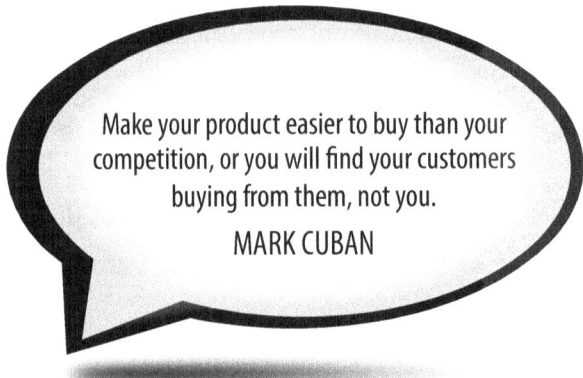

Make your product easier to buy than your competition, or you will find your customers buying from them, not you.

MARK CUBAN

#18
DIRECT MAIL

Direct mail is the best offline media for your advertising dollars. Reason being, you can target your market much better with direct mail than any other media.

If you run television or radio ads, you run the risk of spending money on far more of the market than you need to reach. Same goes for newspapers and magazines. You are reaching readers who may have no interest at all in you and you are paying big bucks to do so.

With direct mail, you can create a database based on your target market and reach out to only those prospects. If you only want to target 500 prospects, you can and will have much more money to spend on those 500 prospects than you would have in other broad reaching mediums.

> It's hard to target a message to a generic 35-year-old middle-class working mother of two. It's much easier to target a message to Jennifer, who has two children under four, works as a paralegal, and is always looking for quick but healthy dinners and ways to spend more time with her kids and less time on housework.
>
> ELIZABETH GARDNER

WAY #19
RINSE AND REPEAT

As with all advertising, repetition is key and direct mail is no different. Sending your message once probably won't produce significant, immediate results.

For a successful direct mail campaign, plan on mailing to the same prospect 5 or 6 times in a 12-month period, and possibly more. Your campaign should also be in addition to other means of advertising to get your message seen in the marketplace.

NOTE: Studies have shown a person must see your message at least NINE times before they will feel anything about it and take action to buy it.

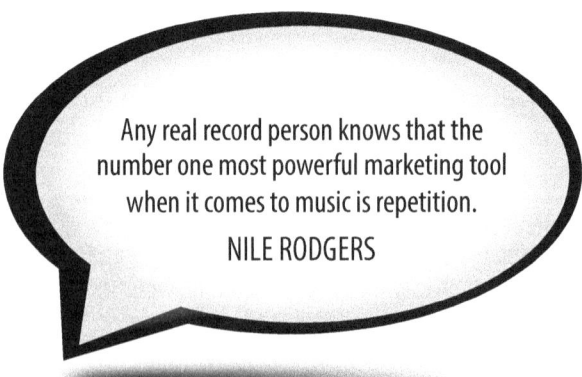

Any real record person knows that the number one most powerful marketing tool when it comes to music is repetition.

NILE RODGERS

WAY #20
SO–THEY SAID "NO"

What should you do after the patient says, "No?"

Review the steps of your presentation.

- Did you know everything about your product/service?
- Did you uncover the patient's need(s)?
- Did you relay the benefits of your product/service in response to their need(s) rather than the features?
- Were you on time, well-groomed, polite, friendly and respectful?
- Did you do anything to turn your prospect off such as knocking the competition, pressuring them to buy, talking more than them?
- Did you ask for the appointment?
- Did you ask when to follow up?

#21
SAY "YES" TO PROSPECTING

Prospecting. Nobody likes to do it, but it is a necessity with all businesses.

One thing to keep in mind, EVERYONE starts out as a prospect.

The more prospects you attract, the more appointments you will have.

Not all prospects are buyers but there could be very good reasons why they won't buy right now.

A good rule of thumb to follow would be to treat every prospect as you would any of your top patients. Tomorrow that prospect may be your new patient.

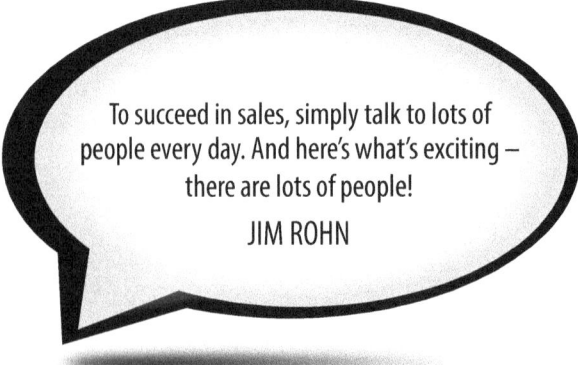

To succeed in sales, simply talk to lots of people every day. And here's what's exciting — there are lots of people!

JIM ROHN

#22

WHO'S A GOOD PROSPECT?

Your best prospects are the ones who resemble your best patients. Analyze the common traits of your best patients to determine who you should be going after as new patients.

Develop a campaign of how to reach these prospects through direct mail, telemarketing and qualifying, and in-person appointments.

Make sure you keep track of your results and tweak your strategy as necessary.

> The aim of marketing is to know and understand the customer so well the product or service fits him and sells itself.
>
> PETER F. DRUCKER

#23
SALES PRESENTATION PITFALLS

Unclear Purpose

Make sure your audience understands why you are making the presentation. Be concise and clear by providing an outline of what you are going to cover.

Unorganization

If your presentation is all over the board, your prospect is not going to be able to follow what you are saying, nor remember what was said. It may also indicate to them that future dealings with you may be just as unorganized and turn them off.

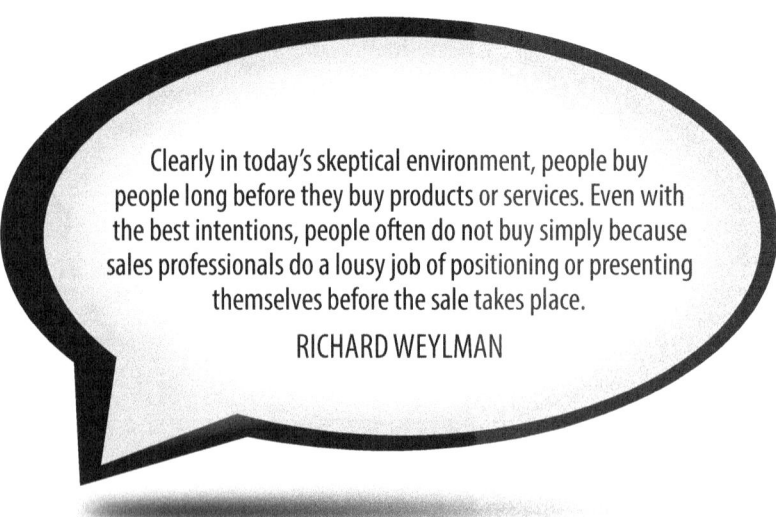

Clearly in today's skeptical environment, people buy people long before they buy products or services. Even with the best intentions, people often do not buy simply because sales professionals do a lousy job of positioning or presenting themselves before the sale takes place.

RICHARD WEYLMAN

#24
MORE SALES PRESENTATION PITFALLS

Too Much Information, Not Enough Benefit Statements
If you are just stating facts and figures, it will become boring to your prospect. Make sure you have qualified your prospect and your presentation is catered to their needs. Then, by turning the features that are important to them into benefits, you will give them the reason(s) to use your practice.

Monotone Voice
If you are monotone in your presentation, it gives your prospect the perception that you are not excited about your product or service. Speak with enthusiasm and confidence. Smile.

Appearance
Your visual appearance will influence your prospect much more than you think. Make sure your clothing is clean, pressed and fits properly. Make sure your shoes are clean and free from nicks and scratches. Women should be sure not to wear jewelry that may be too distracting. Men should be sure their pockets are empty of loose change and keys.

Most important of all-BE RESPECTFUL OF THEIR TIME
Nothing shows more disrespect for your potential patient than being late for their initial appointment. Of course, sometimes this cannot be avoided, but it should be the exception, not the norm.

MAKE IT EASY TO SAY "YES"

Improve your treatment plan conversion rate by making some simple changes in your presentations.

Sometimes when you provide too many options to a patient they get confused and often decide not to buy anything at all.

The best thing to do is to not make anyone have to think about your plan. If they have to think too much, you may lose the sale.

The easier and simpler you can make it for them to make a decision, the better.

If you are selling multiple plans, position your plans as a "Best Option," "Better Option," or "Good Option."

When advertising retail items, focus on only one or two offers or one offer per category.

When creating price points for packages of goods, make one price an obvious choice.

#26
IMPROVE RESPONSE RATES

There are many ways to improve the success rate of direct mail campaigns. Although direct mail is our focus here, many of these strategies can be transferred to other marketing mediums. Think about how you might be able to convert these ideas to advertising you are using now.

Give a FREE gift to increase response.

Make your offer easy to respond to.

Take a look at what your competition is doing and do the opposite or something different.

Make sure the design of your piece goes with your subject matter.

Check with the post office on rules and regulations before designing your piece.

Eliminate risk by offering a rock solid guarantee or a free trial period.

Make sure your copy is in plain English. No industry jargon.

Invest in a copywriter and graphic designer for a higher response.

Benefits are the reason to buy. Make sure you list these rather than features.

More benefits will get you better results. Put them in the P.S., on the envelope, and in the main body copy.

#27
TIPS FOR GREAT SALES LETTERS

When constructing a two-page letter, end the first page in the middle of a sentence to encourage continuing to the next page.

Your offer should be the most prominent copy on the piece.

Start selling immediately. Do not use background information or lead-in copy.

Encourage immediate action. Make sure you use deadlines.

Tell your prospect what you want them to do.

People open envelopes from the back. Stuff the envelope so the material inside faces the back and the writing is facing out.

For your headlines, use lower case type or a combination of upper and lower case type. Do not use all caps. Not only does this come across as "shouting," word-shapes are lost when capitals are used and these shapes add interest to the type and make it much easier to read. It takes much longer to read something that is set in all caps and this can easily turn your prospect off.

#28
BUILD MORE PATIENT LOYALTY

Building patient loyalty should be a plan all practices have.

We all know it is less costly to maintain an old patient than to obtain a new patient.

Strategize on ways to improve your patient retention and loyalty and you will definitely increase your profits.

To build and retain a loyal patient base, you need a few things:

- Multiple products for the same patient
- Highly exceptional customer service
- Product differentiation from that of your competitors
- Higher-end products where price is not an issue

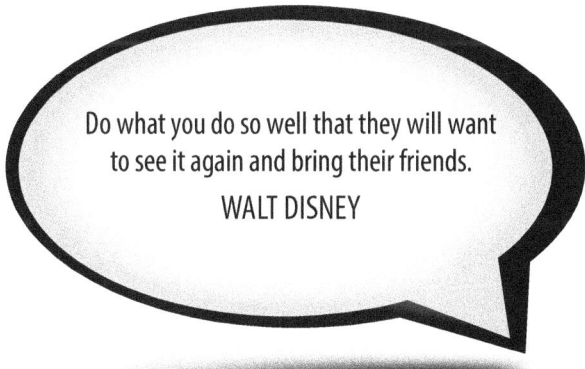

Do what you do so well that they will want to see it again and bring their friends.
WALT DISNEY

#29
EVERYONE LOVES "FREE"

People LOVE to get things for FREE. Often times they will pay a premium price for a more expensive item just to get a freebie.

Several industries have used this strategy for years. Cosmetics is one and is in every department store on any given day– such as buy $28.50 of Lancome products, get a free make-up bag filled with trial size products.

Instead of discounting your product, throw in something for free.

Make a customer, not a sale.
KATHERINE BARCHETTI

#30
GAIN PATIENT CONFIDENCE

Gaining patient confidence is among the top sales advancers. When a patient is indecisive, skeptic, indifferent, or confused it is a breeding ground for losing the sale.

It's important you project an image of experience, dependability, quality and customer service to your prospective patients in order to gain their confidence in you and your practice.

If they don't see the reasons and the advantages to do business with you, they may be hesitant to commit and decide to go elsewhere.

Another way to gain patient confidence is to dispel distrust by offering warranties, patient testimonials, and references. It is also helpful to make your prospects aware of professional organizations that you belong to such as Chamber of Commerces or Dental Associations.

This will give your prospective patient good feelings about your company and help to establish great rapport.

#31
USE CROSS-OVER PROMOTIONS

Cross-over promotions can be a powerful marketing technique. And the beauty of it is the low cost.

Work with other companies who have similar client or patient profiles as yours and you can both tap into each other's customer base.

Here is an example of how it could work.

Let's say you are a dental practice and your "partner"company is a photography studio. At your cleaning/exams, you offer $50 off a portrait session from Acme Photography. Then when Acme Photography has a portrait session with their clients, they offer "Free Whitening for Life", from your practice. It is a win-win for both. Those with clean teeth may want a professional photo and those getting their photo taken may want whiter teeth.

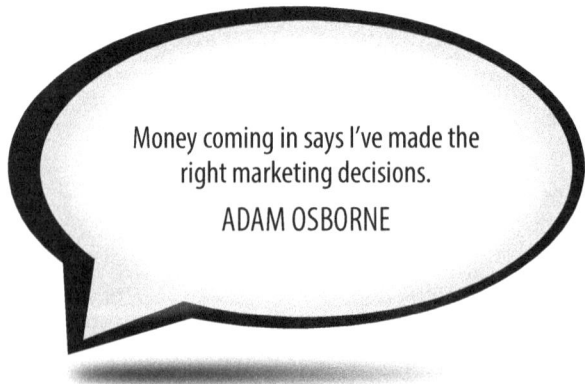

Money coming in says I've made the right marketing decisions.

ADAM OSBORNE

#32
USE DEADLINES

One of the biggest obstacles in closing a sale is procrastination. It is a natural human tendency to postpone and delay decisions.

The best way to combat this is with a deadline. Inject a sense of urgency into your sales presentation, direct mail piece, or display ad whether it be a price increase, limited time offer, limited availability or other reason.

Prospects need some type of incentive to motivate them to get off the fence and take action now.

> Every word, sentence, and headline should have one specific purpose – to lead your potential customer to your order page.
>
> SHELLEY LOWERY

#33
USE LIMITED TIME ONLY

People want what they can't have, so create a sense of urgency with limited availability or limited time offers.

Think of all the hot new toys and gadgets that come out each holiday season. Ever notice there is always a "limited" supply available? And, people camp out overnight just to be one of the lucky ones to grab the product. The manufacturer has created demand by limiting its supply and people flock to the calling.

If there were an unlimited supply, there would be no sense of urgency and less demand for the product. Surely the manufacturer could make more. But this "not enough to go around" tactic creates the demand and the marketing buzz that sells the product.

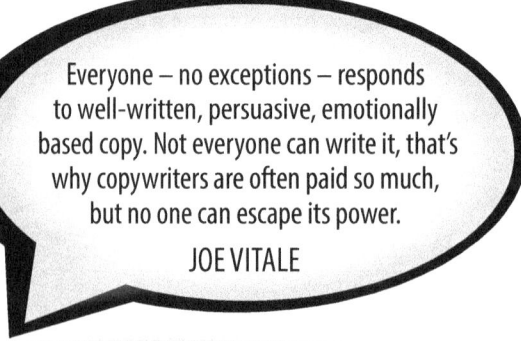

Everyone – no exceptions – responds to well-written, persuasive, emotionally based copy. Not everyone can write it, that's why copywriters are often paid so much, but no one can escape its power.

JOE VITALE

#34
STATE COMMON OBJECTIONS

If you know your product or service has one or two common objections people typically state, don't try to hide them when making a presentation to a new prospect.

Bring it out in the open and overcome it. You know they are probably thinking about it. It could very well be the reason they choose to go with your competitor, without ever telling you the real reason.

Strive for excellence, not perfection.
JACKSON BROWN, JR.

#35
ASK, ASK, ASK FOR REFERRALS

Referrals are one of the best lead sources and you can get them at any time.

Ask for a referral when you don't make the sale. Perhaps you couldn't help this patient but they probably know someone you could help. It may even make your prospect feel better because although they didn't choose you, they can still help you by referring you business.

The best time to get a referral is when people are basking in the glory of their visit with you. They are more willing to help you because you just helped them.

It also helps them to justify their reason for choosing you in the first place. If it is good enough for them, it will be good enough for their closest friends and family. Your patient will want to "brag" to their friends about what a great practice you have and how your service might benefit them too.

Also, don't forget to ask for a referral after you have given terrific service. This could be pre-sale, post-sale or even during the sales process. When you have done something above and beyond, people are truly grateful and more willing to help.

#36
GET AND USE TESTIMONIALS

Everyone should be using testimonials in their marketing. On your web site, in your brochures, on your walls... wherever you can apply them, do.

What others say about you is far more convincing than what you say about yourself.

Patients will also say things that you probably wouldn't say yourself because of modesty and overall credibility. When a patient says it rather than you, there is reason to believe.

The easiest and most direct way to get patient testimonials is to ASK.

Right after the visit or when you are following up, ask your patient if they would please give you a written testimonial. Be sure to let them know that you will be using it in your marketing so you have their permission to use what they say about you.

Always be in the "collecting testimonial mode" so your testimonials are fresh and relevant.

#37
MORE ON TESTIMONIALS

Always use real testimonials and not made-up ones. We can all think of testimonials we have read that just don't seem to be real or believable for that matter.

Whenever you can, use the patient's full name (city and state or company name if appropriate) and be sure you have written permission! Using just a first name and last initial just isn't as convincing and may even be perceived as fake even though it is very real.

One or two word testimonials aren't credible enough and don't have much substance to tell your value.

What do you think when you see these type of testimonials?
   "...terrific!"
   "...truly fantastic!"
   "...I love it..."

Looks either to be edited down or fake, but definitely not credible.

Get your patients to talk about what your service has done for them, how it has helped solve a problem, save money, made them look better, etc. The more specific, the more believable, and the more beneficial to your prospects.

#38
EVEN MORE ON TESTIMONIALS

A great way to get patient testimonials is through the use of an evaluation form. Every time you complete a service or sale, give, email, or send an evaluation form.

Be sure your form asks those questions that will be beneficial for your future marketing use. Asking a few open-ended questions will help to do this.

Also, don't forget to ask permission to use their comments somewhere on the form.

What if you get a great, specific, glowing testimonial but the patient does not want you to use his name? As long as you have other testimonials with names, it's o.k. to have one or two with "name withheld by request".

Most people understand that some people like their privacy and this should not take away from the great things the anonymous patient had to say.

#39

WHAT MAKES A GREAT REFERRAL?

Make sure when asking for referrals that you know what makes a great referral for your practice.

Instead of saying, "Do you know anyone that could use my service?" Rephrase it in a way that is more specific. Such as, "We are looking for new patients who are interested in the most advanced techniques in their oral health care, would you happen to know of anyone?"

With this information, your referee has more specific information, will go through their mental rolodex, and perhaps recall recent conversations where someone expressed concerns with their oral health.

Loyal customers, they don't just come back, they don't simply recommend you, they insist that their friends do business with you.

CHIP BELL

#40
GET REFERRALS IN UNOBVIOUS PLACES

Another source of referrals besides your patients might be other businesses that complement yours.

Offer incentives to businesses for any referrals sent your way.

For instance, you may consider giving $XX gift cards to photographers, wedding related businesses, sports related businesses, daycares, etc. For every gift card that comes back to you, you give that business $XX for the referral.

Another source of referrals besides your patients would be to set up a fundraiser with a church or charity.

Offer to donate a percentage of all proceeds obtained with the fundraiser, a great way to give back and also obtain new patients at the same time.

This could also get you free publicity if orchestrated properly.

#41
THE CUSTOMER IS STILL WHY YOU EXIST

Remember without satisfied customers, you would have no business.

Here are some quick tips to better your customer service.

Go the Extra Mile. Under promise and over deliver. When someone goes out of their way for you, you can't think enough of them.

Treat your patients like you would treat your best friend.

Always have an attitude of gratitude. If you treat your patients like they are a number they will sense it.

Never look at your patient as an interruption and GET RID of anyone in your practice who does.

Make sure there is a process for handling complaints and take care of them in a timely fashion. There is nothing more aggravating than a lack of response when there is an issue. If not handled timely, frustration will build until the patient no longer wants to do business with you, <u>AND</u> then tells everyone they know about it.

Make sure your rules and policies are not turning people away or making it difficult to do business with you.

#42
THE CUSTOMER IS STILL WHY YOU EXIST

One way to make your practice stand out is to address what your patients don't like about your industry.

Let's use a grocery store as an example. Here are some common things people don't like—

Advertised specials not available, baggers not available, counter help not in sight, long check out lines.

To set themselves apart, they could adopt a "Customer Bill of Rights" (posted throughout the store and advertised). The "Bill of Rights" would address each issue listed and what they are doing about it.

Of course much attention would need to be paid to the execution of this "Bill of Rights" but when done, this would not only improve customer service, but would create patients for life.

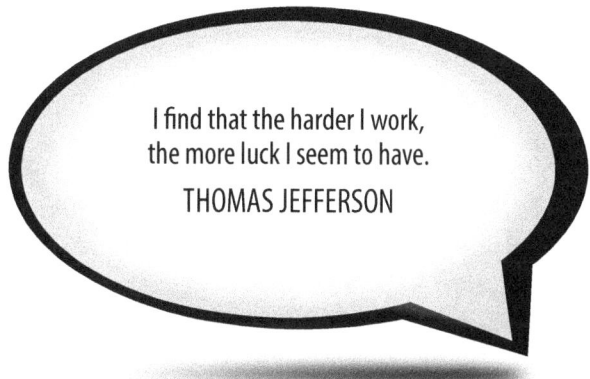

I find that the harder I work, the more luck I seem to have.

THOMAS JEFFERSON

#43
DIFFERENTIATE TO WIN

If there is not much difference between you and your competition, there is no compelling reason for your patient to be loyal to you and they will easily go somewhere else.

These four things happen when there is no difference between you and your competition–

1. Extreme Competitiveness
2. Thinning Margins
3. Less Patient Loyalty
4. Buying Decisions Made on Price

Differentiating yourself from your competition is essential for your practice to prosper.

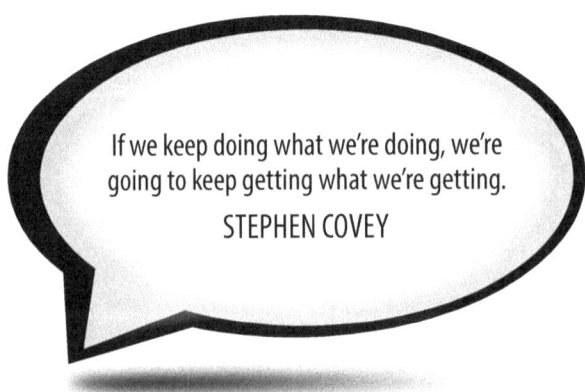

If we keep doing what we're doing, we're going to keep getting what we're getting.
STEPHEN COVEY

#44
THE GIFT OF GAB

On-going effective communication with your patients can be one way to differentiate yourself and create patient loyalty.

Here are five ways you can keep communication flowing between you and your patients:

1. Send a monthly printed newsletter
2. Offer specials/discounts via regular mail, email or your newsletter
3. Offer them offer thanks for their business with a special gift of recognition
4. Send thank you cards after their visit
5. Recognize your patient's birthday with a card and either a free gift or special offer.

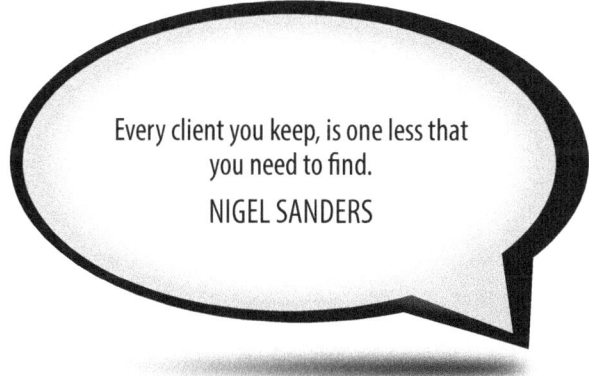

Every client you keep, is one less that you need to find.

NIGEL SANDERS

WAY #45
INCREASE YOUR AVERAGE SALE

Three Ways to Increase Your Average Sale

1. **Bundle your offerings.** Encourage patients to spend more by giving them a package deal on multiple products. Fast food restaurants do this well with their "value" meals that include sandwich, fries, and drink.

2. **Add-on to the sale.** One way to do this is to create a check list of related products or services and when your patient buys that product, you suggest the correlating items. Amazon.com is a good example of this technique. When you order a book, they suggest several other books of similar content or subject matter.

3. **Create sales challenges or goals.** Focus on a product of the week or month for your team to sell. Offer incentives to top producers.

WAY #46
FIND MORE PROSPECTS

Here are a couple ways to find new prospects to target for a direct mail campaign.

You can use a list broker and provide them with all the demographics of your patient such as; household income, age, gender, own home or rent, home value, age of home, etc.

You can also rent lists from publications. For instance, if you know the majority of your patients like to cook and make fine meals, Bon Apetit may be a good source. Or, perhaps many of your patients follow sports closely, a list of subscribers to Sports Illustrated magazine may be a good source.

> In marketing I've seen only one strategy that can't miss - and that is to market to your best customers first, your best prospects second and the rest of the world last.
>
> JOHN ROMERO

#47
INVOLVE YOUR PATIENTS

There is great power in self-discovery through patient involvement during your treatment plan presentation.

When you allow the patient to participate by guiding them to discover the feature or benefit on their own, they will be more inclined to believe it rather than if you did the show and tell for them. They will know what you said works because they did it for themselves. It's now more ingrained in their memory too.

A good example is when you shop for a new car.

Nothing is more compelling than the smell and feel of the new leather and the test drive. If the salesperson drove the car for you it would definitely change the experience and most likely the outcome of the sale.

48
COMMODITIES TO "EXPERIENCE"

Most of the things we buy for want, not need. Needs are commodities like food, shelter, and clothing. Most people don't want to pay much for commodities. But change a commodity into an experience and you can get premium pricing.

Let's use steak as an example. You could buy steak at the store for about $9.99 per pound. You could go to a chain restaurant like Applebee's and get a 12- ounce steak for $14.99 which brings the cost to about $20 per pound or you could go to an upscale steakhouse like Morton's where the cost could be upwards of $70 per pound. The difference between all of these (besides maybe a grade or two on the beef) is the experience.

Make your clients or patients want what you have by creating an unforgettable experience.

Customer experience Is the
new advertising department.
MAX KALEHOFF

#49
GO WHERE YOUR PEOPLE ARE

The thing to keep in mind when searching for lists or places to advertise is that the obvious might not always be the best source. If you are trying to reach sales professionals, logically you might consider *Selling* magazine, but thinking about your customer a bit more might lead you to other places to find those people, such as *Golf* magazine, or magazines on travel, skydiving, skiing, etc.

If you are selling sales training, you may be lost in the ads of *Selling* magazine where there could be a sea of sales training ads. But, you probably would stand out in *Golf* magazine where many of ads there are golf related.

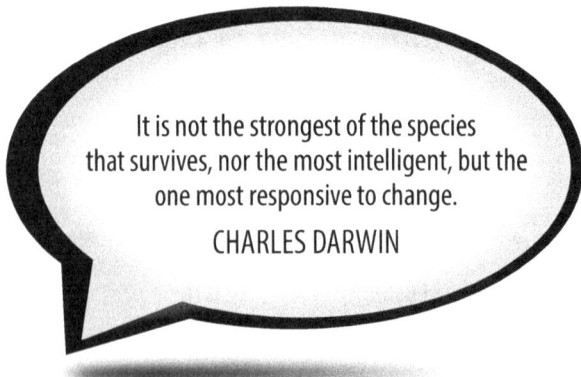

It is not the strongest of the species that survives, nor the most intelligent, but the one most responsive to change.

CHARLES DARWIN

#50
MARKETING 101: THE WHO & THE WHAT

There are four important things to have in place when marketing your business.

1. The Who
2. The What
3. The How
4. The Results

The Who is who you are targeting your message to. This should be to those folks that are a carbon copy of your best patients.

Take a look at your patient history, and segment out those patients who give you your most profitable business. What do they all have in common? This is the audience you want to target.

The What is your advertising message.

What are you trying to get your prospect to do, think, feel or be about your practice? Make sure this message is patient-centered and not about you.

The more exciting and different your message is, the better chance it will get noticed.

We see over 3,000 advertising messages each day. It is essential your message stands out among them.

#51
MARKETING 101: THE HOW & THE RESULTS

The How is the way in which your advertising message is going to be delivered.

We have determined who our potential prospects are from researching our database, we have crafted our marketing message to them, now we need to figure out the best way to reach them.

Is it direct mail, broadcast radio/tv, direct response tv/radio, marriage mail (like Valpak), display ads in newspapers or magazines, on-line advertising, faxing, emailing, tradeshows, networking, etc.?

The very best way is usually through some combination of these different outlets to be sure your message is seen, and seen more than once.

The Results of your advertising are critical in knowing where to spend your advertising dollars. If you run an ad and have no way to measure the results, you do not know whether it is a good medium or not.

Large corporations advertise this way. They do brand building that is not trackable. But when you have limited dollars to spend, it is important you know you are getting business from those dollars.

Using a unique offer or a coupon that must be redeemed, a special phone extension, or person's name to ask for are ways to track advertising. At the very least make sure you ask, "How did you hear about us?"

#52
TIPS FOR MORE PROFITS

Should you Fire your Patients?

Take a close look at all of your accounts. There are most likely patients who are high maintenance causing you to use up a lot of time and resources, resulting in little or no profit. A better idea might be to fire these patients and focus on those patients who appreciate your efforts and are profitable to your practice.

Hold Weekly Meetings:

It's important to monitor what's going on in the practice and hold your staff accountable. Discuss best practices, do some role-playing, and keep them motivated.

> In sales there are going to be times when you can't make everyone happy. Don't expect to and you won't be disappointed. Just do your best for each client in each situation as it arises. Then, learn from each situation how to do it better the next time.
>
> TOM HOPKINS

#53
EMAIL: ANOTHER TOOL IN THE BOX

The allure of the relatively low cost of email marketing makes people want to abandon their print advertising and send everything via email.

In email marketing, an open rate of 20% is very good. But there are more and more spam filters being added to email servers making it increasingly difficult to get email delivered.

Email anyway, but do it in conjunction with off-line types of marketing.

People easily delete emails especially when they are busy. With a printed flyer, newsletter or sales letter they can hold them aside and read them when convenient making it much more valuable, despite the higher cost.

Every contact we have with a customer influences whether or not they'll come back. We have to be great every time or we'll lose them.

KEVIN STIRTZ

#54
DON'T CUT PRICES – BUNDLE

Many businesses cut prices as a response to increasing competitive pressure. The only thing this will do is shorten your business' lifespan.

See where you might be able to bundle your products and services together to offer more value thereby providing more of your product than may have been typically purchased. With bundling, you can increase prices and give value at same time.

> You've got to look for a gap, where competitors in a market have grown lazy and lost contact with the readers or the viewers.
>
> RUPERT MURDOCH

#55
SMART WAYS TO USE VOICEMAIL

Smarter Ways to Use Voicemail and Get Your Messages Returned-

- Give the person a reason to call back by providing something that may peak their interest to encourage a call back. But don't give them ALL the information or there will be no reason to call back.

- State your phone number clearly and slowly. You may even want to repeat your number twice.

- Don't ask them to return your call at a specific time. This is asking too much and may even come off the wrong way.

- Never leave a message saying that you plan to call them back. This definitely gives them a reason not to return your call.

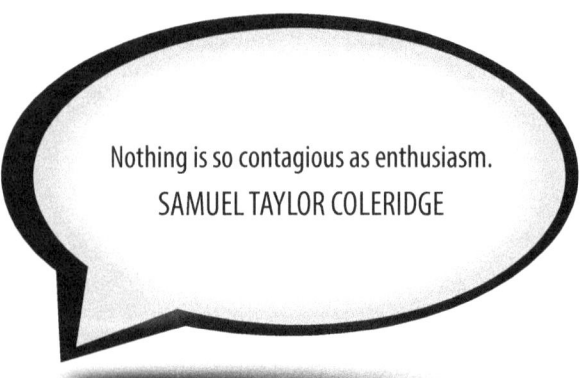

Nothing is so contagious as enthusiasm.
SAMUEL TAYLOR COLERIDGE

#56
TARGET YOUR MESSAGE

Many businesses make the mistake and design their marketing messages to broadly appeal to everyone. But what happens when you do this is often the opposite. When you use a broad approach there are no distinguishing benefits and your prospect won't see why they should choose you over your competitor.

Target your messages to attract your ideal customer. If you sell gourmet pizza, you want your message targeting those people who care about quality ingredients and gastronomic experiences, not cheap pizza. Using a broad approach in this instance will most likely attract all the wrong customers and very few of the right customers.

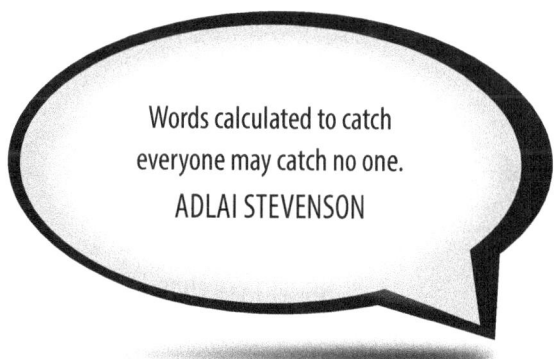

Words calculated to catch everyone may catch no one.
ADLAI STEVENSON

#57
FEAR NOT– STAY FOCUSED

When the economy goes crazy as it does every so many years, those businesses who do well realize they can't allow what's going on around them to change their focus or create fear.

But those who may have already been experiencing lack from situations created prior, without anything to do with current economic woes, become fearful pulling their money out of their investments (whether it is marketing or personal) and carry on with a dismal view of the future. FEAR will immobilize you if you let it.

It's important to stay focused on your goals and not abandon them because of what might happen in the future. Forge ahead with whatever marketing you've been doing that is bringing in business.

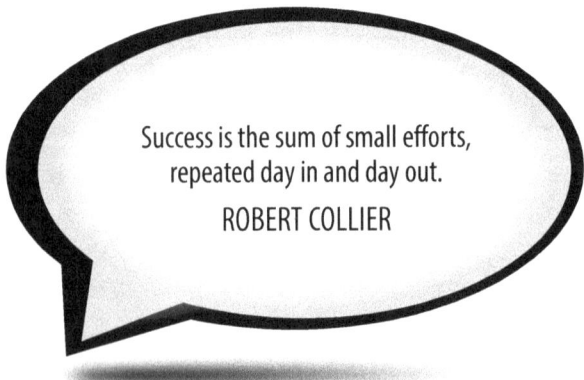

Success is the sum of small efforts, repeated day in and day out.

ROBERT COLLIER

#58
CRITICAL COPY

It has been said that an ad is salesmanship in print. What a salesperson does in a face-to-face meeting is create and react to the customer's emotions to get them to buy.

Print ads, flyers, emails, newsletters, etc. can evoke emotions just like a salesperson.

Choosing your copy is critical in getting response to your sales messages. You must appeal to your prospect by getting into what's going on in their world, feeling their pain, solving their problems, etc.

When you thoroughly know your prospect and what they're thinking you can craft your copy accordingly and sell more product.

Top-flight sales copy is never a cost. It's a profit center."

CLAYTON MAKEPEACE

#59
NO PAIN – NO GAIN

One of the best ways to evoke emotion in your prospect and get them to respond is to identify the "pain" they are experiencing and then offer the "solution" to eliminate that pain.

If you watch TV infomercials they are very good at doing this and it is good to study them for their marketing value.

Infomercials not only bring up the pain, they also have multiple testimonials of people who experienced the exact same pain and then expound on how the product cured all of their ills.

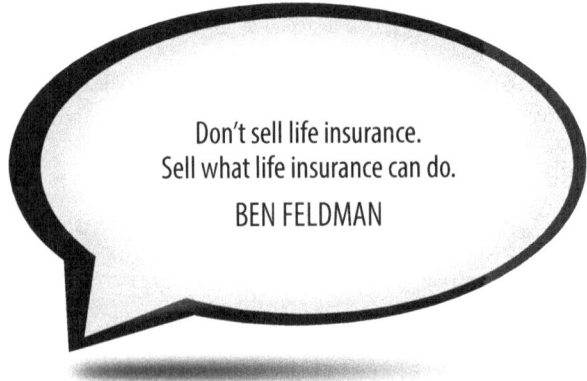

Don't sell life insurance.
Sell what life insurance can do.
BEN FELDMAN

#60
APPEALING TO EMOTIONS

In sales copy, appealing to people's emotions is important.

Here is a short list of how people want to feel when they purchase something:

- stress-free
- youthful, energetic, healthy
- status elevation among their peers
- secure
- saving time
- look good and feel good

In a nutshell, they just want to feel better than they did before the purchase.

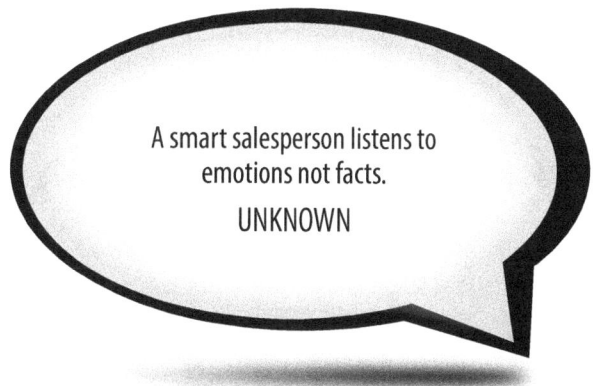

A smart salesperson listens to emotions not facts.

UNKNOWN

#61
GET NOTICED

Press releases can be a great way to get free promotion. But it is increasingly difficult to get the media's attention.

Here are some ways that might help get your press release noticed.

- First and foremost what you send must be NEWS. The existence of your practice is not news.

- The headline of your release should have a HOOK. It should appeal to human interest, solve a problem, contain some drama, or a local connection. If you can connect with a celebrity, you are almost sure to get attention. People love reading about celebrities and the media loves reporting on them.

- Focus on something already in the news. For example, connecting to what's going on in a poor economy and offering a solution may garner attention.

- Do something outrageous or different than what everyone else in your industry is doing.

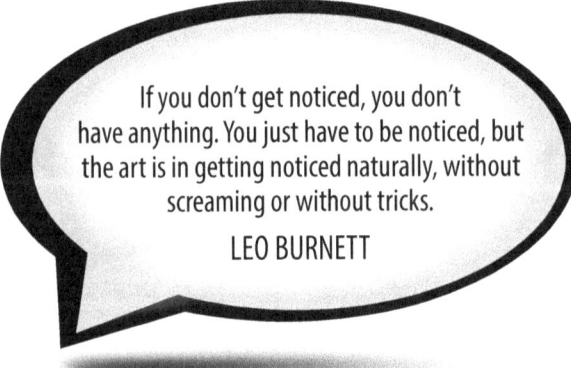

If you don't get noticed, you don't have anything. You just have to be noticed, but the art is in getting noticed naturally, without screaming or without tricks.

LEO BURNETT

#62

GET MORE NOTICED

Instead of using the traditional press release format, a better approach may be to write a "pitch" letter giving them the idea of the story, the facts and the sources.

Editors are busy and don't have time to weed through all the fluff of a typical press release. Be as concise as possible. Use bullets to stress the key points to make it fast and easy for them to see if there is something of value to their readers.

Timing is everything. If your topic is "hot," bring this to their attention first thing and let them know you have the sources for them.

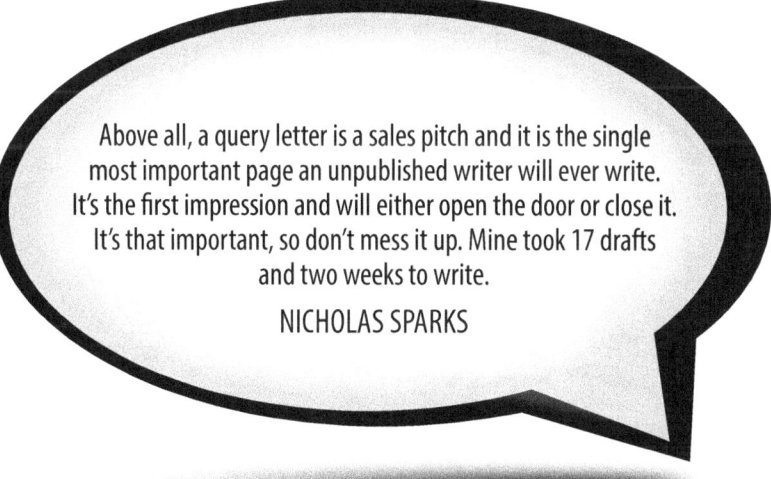

Above all, a query letter is a sales pitch and it is the single most important page an unpublished writer will ever write. It's the first impression and will either open the door or close it. It's that important, so don't mess it up. Mine took 17 drafts and two weeks to write.

NICHOLAS SPARKS

#63
YOU ARE THE STAR

Injecting personality into your marketing will increase your results. It will also make you stand out from your competition.

When your advertising and marketing is more personal it is much more interesting to whoever is reading it.

The best way to do this is to write your ads, sales letters, thank you notes as if you are writing a personal note to one of your good friends. Don't worry so much about the language you use. Use the same words you would use when speaking to a friend one-on-one.

The idea is to be yourself and not the stuffy, boring things most people see from everyone else. Make it fun and worth attention!

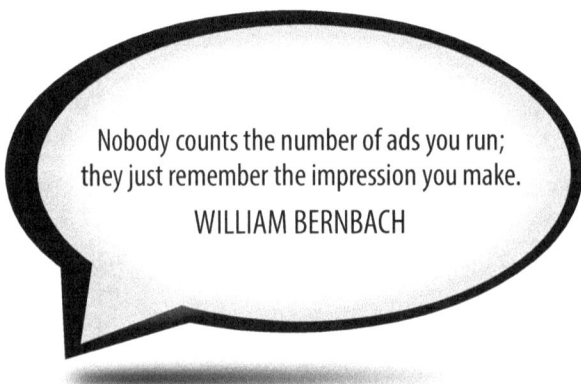

Nobody counts the number of ads you run; they just remember the impression you make.

WILLIAM BERNBACH

#64
TO MARKET... EVERYDAY

When is the best time to market your business? The answer is ALL the time. Thinking of cutting your marketing during an economic downturn? Think again.

From 1980 to 1985, McGraw-Hill Research analyzed 600 companies and their marketing spend. Their conclusions were that those companies who had maintained or increased their advertising during the recession in 1981 and 1982 commanded an average sales growth of 275% over the next five years after 1985 when the economy improved. Those companies that slashed their advertising obtained a mere 19% growth rate over the same time period.

The moral of the story is find another expense to cut instead of your advertising!

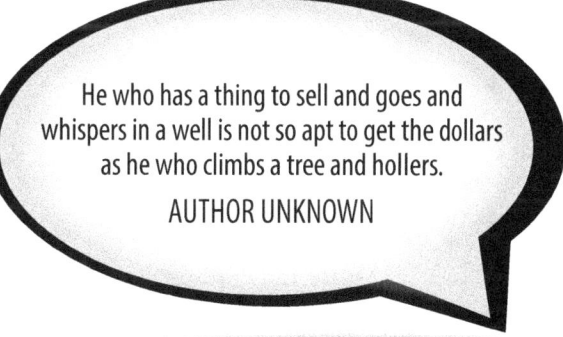

He who has a thing to sell and goes and whispers in a well is not so apt to get the dollars as he who climbs a tree and hollers.

AUTHOR UNKNOWN

#65
SWEAT THE SMALL STUFF

What is really important to all businesses is customer retention.

More often than not it is the little things that turn a patient away.

The small stuff that makes the difference between choosing say, one hotel over another. It could be the desk clerk that remembers you and greets you by name. It could be the impeccably clean bathroom. It could be the bellman that is always at attention at the front door upon your departures and arrivals. It may be the smile from the housekeeper in the hallway. Little things add up to big things and everlasting impressions as well as good feelings.

Take a look at all the little things you do and see where you can improve so your patients feel good about doing business with you and want to come back for more.

The goal as a company is to have customer service that is not just the best, but legendary.

SAM WALTON

#66
WHY YOU EXIST & WHAT MAKES YOU SPECIAL?

What are your competitive advantages?

Every practice has these. It is most likely the reason you started your practice or what your practice has morphed into as a result. It is what separates you from everyone else in your industry. And what brings patients to your door, phone, or web site.

Knowing your competitive advantages is one thing but making your patients and prospects aware of them could mean the difference between double digit growth and closing up shop.

To capitalize on of your competitive advantages, it's important to focus your marketing messages on what makes you unique.

General statements about you being the best, the fastest, the newest, etc. are meaningless. Be specific. "Drill" down to what it is that makes you special and market it at every opportunity.

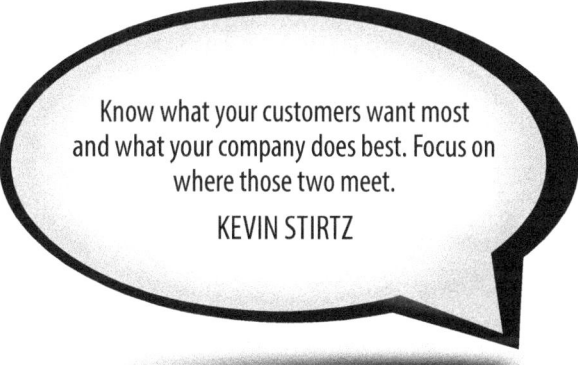

Know what your customers want most and what your company does best. Focus on where those two meet.

KEVIN STIRTZ

#67
USE THAT P.O.P.

One of the best investments for a practice is in point-of-purchase displays (P.O.P.) and messages placed in patient areas.

Product displays allow you to dramatically increase the impact your product has at the time it counts most—purchase time. This is especially true if you have impulse or convenience items that cost little and don't require much thought to purchase.

Don't let the fact you do not have such items discourage you from displaying your information. Patients do not know nor do they remember all you do. You need to keep them informed. A poster, rack card, display tent or brochure placed in conspicuous areas can be a tremendous opportunity to get more business.

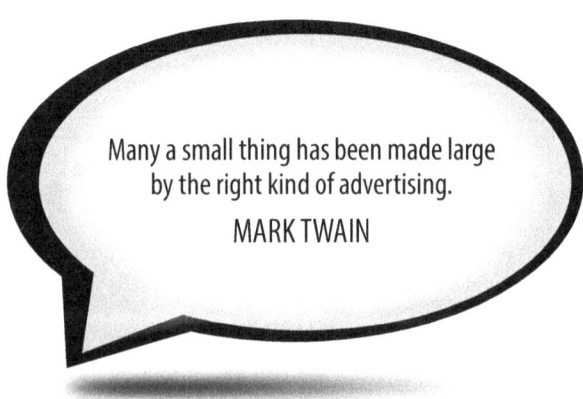

Many a small thing has been made large by the right kind of advertising.

MARK TWAIN

#68
TRAITS OF GREAT SALESPEOPLE

- Great salespeople are goal setters. They know what they want and make a plan to get it.

- Great salespeople are persistent. They don't let obstacles get in the way of their success.

- Great salespeople ask good questions. They know that asking good questions will give them the information they need to make the best presentation of their product.

- Great salespeople listen to what the prospect/customer has to say. They let the customer do most of the talking.

- Great salespeople have genuine enthusiasm and passion. They love their product and their company and it is contagious to their customer.

- Great salespeople take responsibilities for their actions. They do not blame others for their situation.

- Great salespeople follow up, repeatedly. They never give up.

- Great salespeople work hard. They don't wait for business to come to them, they go out and get it.

#69
HE SAID "WHAT?"

Patient feedback is vital to your business. Consider devising some sort of form or survey to follow up on recent visits. It is a great way to have open dialogue with your visits.

Here are a couple things you can glean from your patient's feedback:

- Confirm that you are meeting all their needs and be able to take care of any situations where that is not happening as quickly as possible.

- Discover other needs your patient may have that you are not addressing, thereby creating new revenue streams.

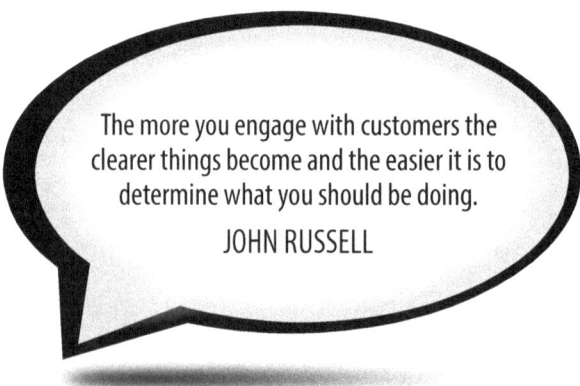

The more you engage with customers the clearer things become and the easier it is to determine what you should be doing.

JOHN RUSSELL

#70
COMPLAINTS = OPPORTUNITY

Patients complaints are a great marketing opportunity.

If you handle complaints quickly, acknowledge the fault was yours (even if it may have been theirs) and compensate your patient, it can go a long way in developing patient loyalty.

Rather than having your patient tell everyone they know about the bad experience they had with your practice, when you handle complaints expediently and efficiently, your patients will be champions to your cause and feel great that you care about them.

> Statistics suggest that when customers complain, business owners and managers ought to get excited about it. The complaining customer represents a huge opportunity for more business.
>
> ZIG ZIGLAR

#71
TREATMENT PLAN FOLLOW UP

So the patient did not schedule their treatment plan. Don't let it end there. Be proactive.

1. Follow up within 48 hours to get conversion. Don't wait your them to call you.

2. Send them a FedEx or Priority Mail package. This will ensure it is opened by your patient.

3. Create a sense of urgency. Reiterate why they need to follow through with their treatment plan.

4. Make sure you include testimonials of patients with their very same issue.

5. Give them a reason to schedule right away.

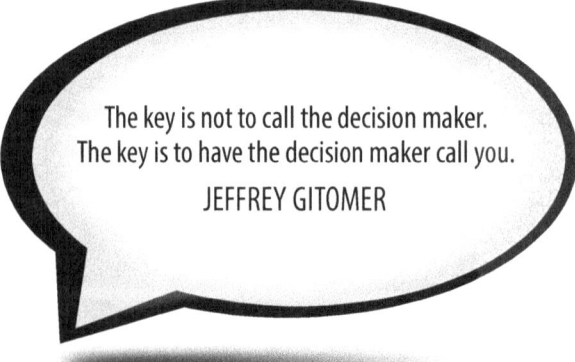

The key is not to call the decision maker.
The key is to have the decision maker call you.

JEFFREY GITOMER

#72

CHANGE THE "WE" TO "YOU"

It's not about YOU. But is a word you need in your marketing.

If your marketing messages talk all about your practice and your services, you are missing the mark. Patients and prospects do not care about you or your practice. What they care about is themselves and their problems and their needs or wants.

Check the wording of your messages and be sure the pronoun that is used is YOU not WE.

In the end, the customer doesn't know, or care, if you are small or large as an organization. She or he only focuses on the garment hanging on the rail in the store.

GIORGIO ARMANI

#73

USE A P.S.

The Most Read Part of a Sales Letter after the Headline...
is the P.S.

People naturally read the headline then jump down to the P.S. before reading the entire letter. When you write your P.S., imagine that the reader will only be reading the headline and the P.S. to help you decide what it should include.

Your P.S. should re-state your offer, remind your prospect of the major benefit, mention your guarantee and give your reader a deadline to act/respond.

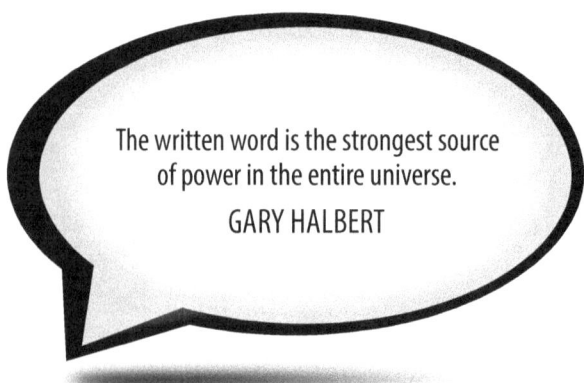

The written word is the strongest source of power in the entire universe.

GARY HALBERT

#74
NEVER, EVER STOP

KEEP YOUR NAME OUT THERE!

The most important strategy you can use at any given time is to be sure you are incorporating some sort of marketing activity on a DAILY basis.

We all have millions of things we need to do each day, but if you let your marketing fall by the wayside you will be risking potential sales, strengthening your competition and most definitely limiting your income.

Remember, when you are out of sight, you are out of mind and you could be out of business.

KEEP MARKETING!

> Many of life's failures are people who did not realize how close they were to success when they gave up.
>
> THOMAS A. EDISON

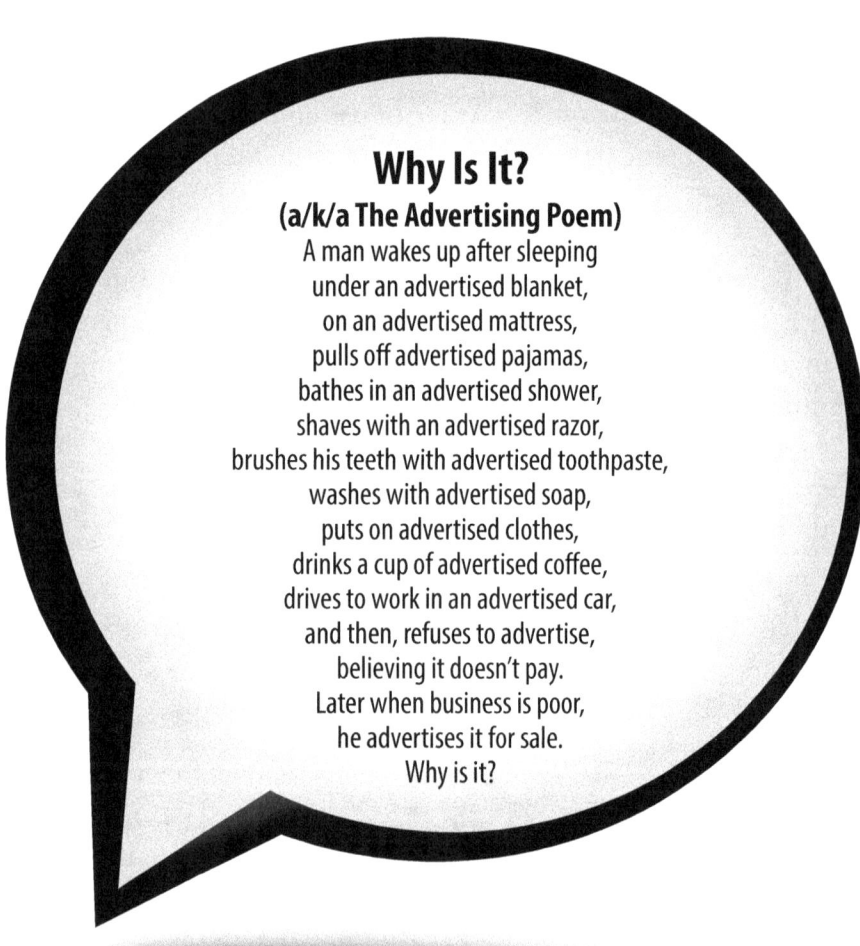

Why Is It?
(a/k/a The Advertising Poem)
A man wakes up after sleeping
under an advertised blanket,
on an advertised mattress,
pulls off advertised pajamas,
bathes in an advertised shower,
shaves with an advertised razor,
brushes his teeth with advertised toothpaste,
washes with advertised soap,
puts on advertised clothes,
drinks a cup of advertised coffee,
drives to work in an advertised car,
and then, refuses to advertise,
believing it doesn't pay.
Later when business is poor,
he advertises it for sale.
Why is it?

www.ingramcontent.com/pod-product-compliance
Lightning Source LLC
Chambersburg PA
CBHW061444180526
45170CB00004B/1556